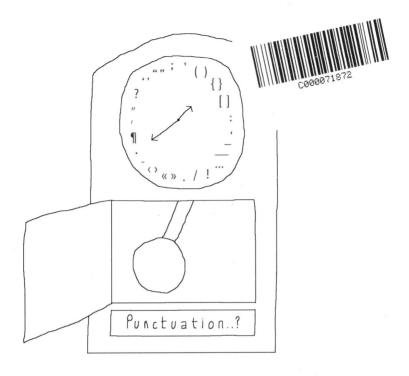

The snake's hisses

Apostrophe '

The most common use of an apostrophe is to indicate *possession* by a person or thing of some other person or thing, for example: John's book or Europe's history.

Using an apostrophe to indicate possession is really quite straightforward, yet it is a frequent source of confusion. There are two separate cases to consider: *singular nouns* and *plural nouns* (a noun is a word used as the name of a person, place or thing).

Singular nouns
When a noun is singular (standing for a single person or thing) we show possession by adding 's. For example:

The snake's hisses   The hisses of one snake

The snakes' hisses

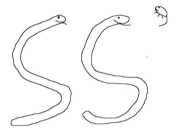

Plural nouns

When a noun is plural (standing for more than one person or thing) we show possession by adding the apostrophe after the final s'. For example:

The snakes' hisses   The hisses of two or more snakes

An exception

As with many rules, there is always an exception. This one concerns nouns that form their plural without adding an s. For example:

Child   Children
Woman   Women
Man   Men

Words like this, take 's in both their forms. For example:

The woman's sadness   The sadness of one woman
The women's celebration   The celebration of two or more women

Be careful to distinguish its from it's. For example:

Its   no apostrophe, is a possessive meaning 'belonging to it', whereas

It's   with an apostrophe is a contraction meaning 'it is':

The umbrella did its job   It's raining

I can't be
bothered
to read
this book

There is
no such
word as
can't

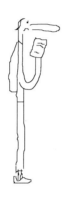 

Another use of the apostrophe is to indicate missing letters in abbreviated words and writing speech (from somebody talking). For example:

Full form	Shortened form
Cannot	Can't
Do not	Don't
Does not	Doesn't
I will	I'll
Is not	Isn't
It is	It's
Let us	Let's
Shall not	Shan't
There is	There's
You are	You're

An apostrophe is not used to make the plural of acronyms (a word formed from the initial letter of other words). For example:

MPS are good for nothing, or dates: in the 1990s.

However, it is used in the possessive:

It was GB's decision.

It can be used in plurals but only when clarity demands it (dot your i's and cross your t's). The apostrophe has largely vanished from company names and other commercial uses (Barclays Bank, Collins Dictionary).

That is all there is to it, practise these simple rules and you will be the apos*trophe* champion.

Brackets: Round/parentheses ( )

Round brackets are the brackets you most often read. They are used to show extra information and words that could be removed without changing the meaning of the sentence and extra information. You use round brackets (also known as parentheses) in the following situations.

- To give an explanation or make an extra comment:

    He had no hesitation in what he was saying (no matter how brutal, loud and offensive it seemed), or in showing how much he hated them ('those stupid pigs').

- To provide a reference or statistic:

    Mr Yob (age 25) was found on the High Street (at 9.30pm).
    He continued to be aggressive and did not cooperate,
    so we took him to the nearest station.

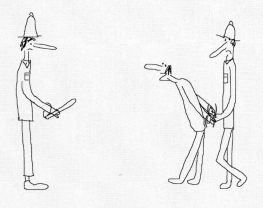

- To indicate optional words that imply some doubt:

  Listen mate (Bobby), you do not want to mess with me.

In mathematics

Round/parenthesis brackets are used to change the order in which mathematical operators are applied:

$5 + 7 \times 2 = 19$ because the multiplication is done before the addition.

$(5 + 7) \times 2 = 24$ because the brackets indicate to do the addition first.

Brackets: Curly/braces { }

Curly brackets are sometimes called braces and are used to indicate a series of equal choices:

What should I have {sausage, cheese, a sandwich, pretzel}? I am not sure...

They can also be used in specialised ways in mathematics and equations (to delimit sets).

Brackets: Square [ ]

Square brackets are used in printed text and writing mainly to establish a different voice, tone, or to provide clarity and enclose information that has been provided by someone other than the writer:

I wish you would let me [Mr Hill] make you reconsider.

Square brackets can also be used with an ellipsis (...) to signal missing material or content:

Frieda said 'Do you remember [...] when we walked through town?'

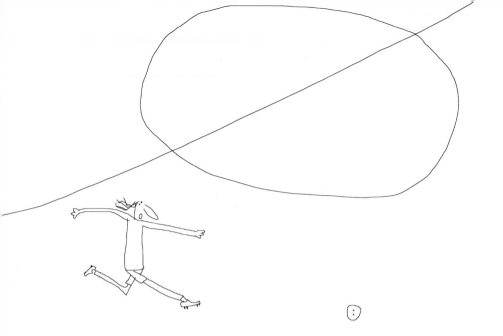

Colon :

Colons are used more in printed text than in general everyday writing. A semicolon (;) links two balanced statements; a colon (:) explains or unpacks the statement or information before it:

> I pegged it straight up the pitch; he was ready to to feed the ball through, but...

> He gave me his explanation: he was picking his nose.

You can also use a colon to introduce a list:

> The following are playing in midfield: Harry Dobbs, Franklin Frank, Marvin Marv and Speedy Steve.

Comma ,

The comma is the punctuation mark most often used in English. It has many functions but all come down to making meaning clearer and/or reflecting a natural pause in the rhythm of the sentence. Commas are used in the following situations.

* To separate items in a list or sequence:

  They decided to order a drink, sit down, then discuss business.

  When did we hook-up last month: Tuesday 20th, Wednesday 21st, Thursday 22nd or Friday 23rd?

* When there is a change in the subject of the sentence:

  I tried to win him over, but he went ahead with his original plans.

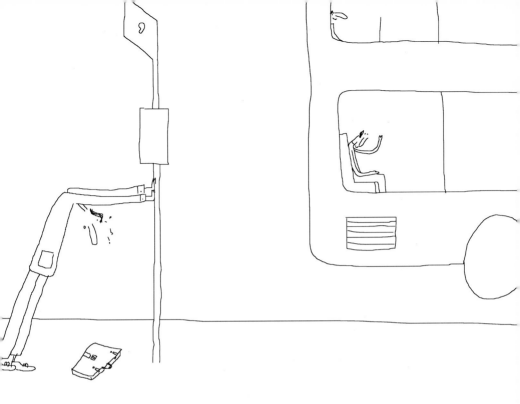

- As a kind of bracket (the parenthetical comma):

  By then, however, I could not go any further and missed the bus.

- To separate a list of adjectives describing the same noun (an adjective is a word giving characteristics to a noun):

  It was a stressful, tiring, unproductive day.

Dash – —

In printed text there are two types of dash: the em dash (—) and en dash
(–). These dashes are both longer than the hyphen (-) which is not a dash.
The em dash with no word space either side (—), is used mainly in America.
The en dash with a word space either side (–) corresponds to the dash in
general use. The main uses of it are as follows.

- To introduce an explanation or expansion of what comes before it:

    Did you know the em dash is twice as long as the en dash – I do now.

- To indicate an aside:

    My girlfriend – who is happy with my en dash – is a language expert.

- To show a numerical range, standing for the word to:

    There were 100–900 cars and it took two hours to cross the road.

Ellipsis ...

The ellipsis is three full stops in a row. It shows that something is missing,
or in the case of conversation, that the speaker has hesitantly come to a halt.

- In quotations, he thought:

    '... I have to wait, maybe something will happen tomorrow.'

    'How long do I have to wait... something will happen tomorrow.'

    'How long do I have to wait, maybe something will happen...'

- In maths, an ellipsis shows that not all the numbers have been given:

    $\pi = 3.14159...$

- In faltering speech:

    I was going to ring you tomorrow, but now I am not sure...

Exclamation mark !

In written speech, an exclamation mark is used to show that something
has been said loudly, or is an expression of shock, anger or outrage. It is also
used to indicate a command telling someone what to do. You see it used in
the following situations.

- To indicate a command or warning:

    A little bit louder!
    Not too loud!

- To show that a strong feeling is being expressed:

    I think it is perfect!
    Remember our youth!

- To demonstrate hope or regret:

  I hope Betty can come!
  She is taken!

The exclamation mark also occurs quite often in literature, especially in poetry, to express a strong feeling or idea:

  Ah! you are wrong, once she sees me cleaned up; washed and shaved, she will find me irresistible!

In everyday writing, the exclamation mark is often overused in the belief that it adds drama and excitement. It is, perhaps, the punctuation mark that should be used with most restraint.

Forward slash /

The forward slash is used as both a way of linking words and numbers and a way of separating them. Here are some examples.

- Linking words:

    The boss/slave relationship was horrendous.

- Representing the word *per* in measurements in non-specialist texts:

    18 miles/hour   18 miles per hour

- Representing the word *or* in non-specialist texts:

    If you have an accident, you must see the nurse/doctor.

An almost identical character to the forward slash is the fraction or division slash (∕) but with more of an angle, it is used to make fractions.

Full stop .

A full stop indicates the end of a sentence, like the one at end of this sentence. It is a small dot placed after the last word and is not needed if the sentence ends with a question mark or an exclamation mark. A full stop is also used after abbreviations:

No. 1   e.g.   i.e.   sec.

But a full stop is not necessary after contractions (abbreviations which end in the same letter as the original word):

Mrs   Mr   Dr   St

Nor is a full stop necessary after capital letters used as acronyms (a word formed from the initial letters of others):

DJ   USA   BBC   MC

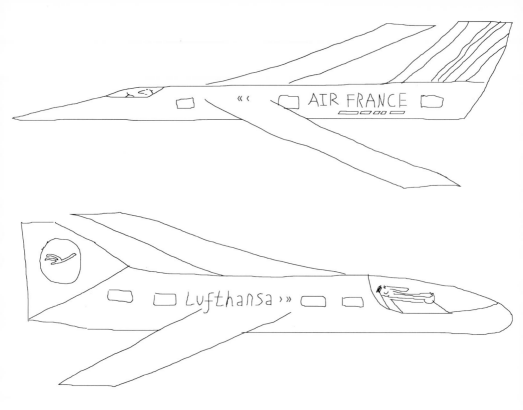

Guillemets « » ‹ ›   » « › ‹

Guillemets are used in several languages to indicate passages of speech
in the same way that single and double quotation marks (' ' " ") are used in
the English language. Guillemets are named after the French font designer
Guillaume Le Bé 1525–1598.

- In French and Italian, the guillemets almost always point out:

    «like so» and ‹like so›

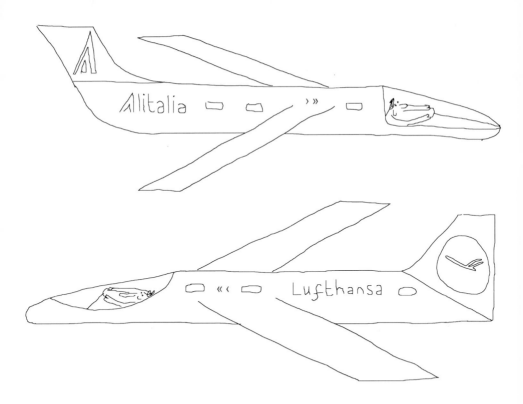

- But in German they more frequently point in:

  »like so« and ›like so‹

Single guillemets should not be confused with angle brackets (⟨ ⟩) nor with the arithmetical symbols meaning less than (<) and greater than (>).

Hyphen -

The hyphen is commonly used to connect parts of compound nouns such as go-getter, and compound adjectives such as up-to-date.

In printed text, the hyphen is shorter than the em dash (—) and en dash (–), but in handwriting there is not usually any distinction made between them. In many fonts, the minus sign is same length as the hyphen but is a different character.

The hyphen's job is to link words and parts of words, including its use at the end of a line to show that the rest of the word is on the next line (hyphenated). In English, the hyphen is generally used as follows.

- To join two or more words to form a new single word:

  Dive-bomb
  x-ray
  Passer-by

- To join two or more words to form a compound adjective:

  'Hello, it is your bank manager here; I need an up-to-the-minute
  account of what you are buying'.

- To join a prefix to a name or designation:

  anti-terrorism   ex-girlfriend

- To indicate a common second element in all but the last word of a list:

  Five-, six- or sevenfold increase in sales.

- To clarify meaning in groups of words which might otherwise be unclear
  or ambiguous:

  Twenty-odd people came to the business meeting.
  The French-speaking people were very interesting.

Interpunct ·

An interpunct is a small dot used to separate words in ancient Latin texts and inscriptions on monuments and buildings. It can also be called an interpoint or middle dot. The dot is vertically centred between the words: USQUE·INTERPUNCT·FREQUENS. Inscriptions on 20th century buildings sometimes use a small triangle, pointing either up or down, instead of the dot form. Our familiar style of using spaces to separate words is much more modern — it appeared sometime around 600–800AD.

Interpuncts (·) should not be used as decimal points, which sit on the line (.) nor confused as bullet points (•) which are much bigger and bolder.

¶ Pilcrow

The pilcrow (an old paragraph sign) is a typographic character commonly used to mark new paragraphs. The pilcrow was used in the Middle Ages (around 3 century) to mark a new line of thought, before the convention of discreetly indented paragraphs was commonplace. ¶ This non-alphabetic symbol varies from typeface to typeface but the design shown here (¶) is normal. It is drawn like a backwards p aligning to the height of the capitals and could also be marked with a full-height cent-like sign (₵).

Pilcrow ¶

A pilcrow is an old scribe mark used to mark the beginning of a paragraph or main text section. It is also occasionally used as a reference mark ¶. ⌐

Prime ' "

Single '
The single prime is used as a symbol for measurement in feet:

$1' = 1$ foot

Double "
The double prime is used as a symbol for measurement in inches:

$12'' = 12$ inches

Primes also have specialist use in chemistry and biology to indicate particular carbon atoms within carbon ring structures and to identify the ends of DNA/RNA strands.

Primes should not be confused with single or double quotation marks (' ' " "), nor with the apostrophe ('), or single or double dumb/straight quotes (' ") from typewriter days and which are commonly found in emails.

Question mark ?

In English, we use a question mark at the end of the text that forms a direct question:

What shall I do today?
What time is it?

You can also use it when the question looks more like a statement:

I am not sure?
I wonder if my brain can help me?
Surely it can?

Tony Blair asked what   he tried to fix it,
the problem was;   didn't he?

And you use a question mark in tag questions:

He tried to fix it, didn't he?

But you do not use a question mark for a reported (indirect) question:

Tony Blair asked what the problem was.

A question mark in brackets can also be used to indicate doubt or uncertain things, locations or dates:

I think that tune was by (?) dubstep DJ Kode9.

The vinyl had a red sticker and blue (?) record sleeve.

“

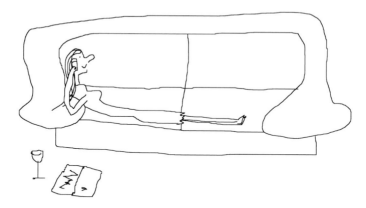

Quotation marks ' ' " "

Quotation marks are used to indicate direct speech and quotations in writing. In handwriting it is common to use double quotation marks (" "). In printed text a distinction is usually made between double (" ") and single (' ') quotation marks. In the UK, single quotation marks are now mainly used and the double quotation marks are reserved for 'quotes within quotes'.

> Lizzy sitting snugly in her sofa, hesitated as she said, 'Should we get somewhere together?'

When reporting direct speech, the closing quotation mark comes after the final full stop or any other punctuation mark that is part of the quotation:

> Max speedily replied, 'I could not think of a better idea!'

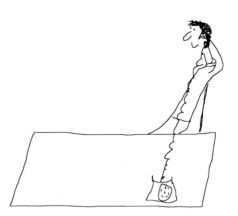

If the reported speech is followed (or interrupted) by a verb (a word indicating an action or occurrence) such as say or shout, the punctuation (usually a comma) dividing the sentence goes inside the first quotation marks:

'I wanted to ask you, but I was too scared,' he said, sitting in his chair.

If the reported word or phrase is at the end of a sentence, the punctuation for the whole sentence is placed outside the quotation marks:

What about 'rent'? Seeing as we are moving in together, we should pay half; that sounds fair.

If a quotation occurs within a quotation, for the quote within the quote, you use double quotation marks:

'The estate agent stated that it would be "not much" at the viewing.'

;

Semicolon ;

Many people find use of the semicolon very confusing; it is the punctuation mark least used in many modern books. But it can be extremely helpful.

Its main role is to indicate a separation between two parts of a sentence that is stronger than a comma but less strong than dividing the sentence in two with a full stop. Normally the two parts (clauses) divided by a semicolon, balance each other (unlike the use of the colon (:) which links or unpacks the two):

She looked at me; I was lost for words.

The semicolon is also very useful when you have a long sentence that already contains commas:

> What came over us? Was it the relaxing time we had on Wednesday, when we were in town; was it my present, the chocolate; or was it just the warm, sunny day of a good summer?

© Copyright 2012 User design (Thomas Bohm).

ISBN: 978-0-9570712-2-3

Research, content development, book design and illustration: Thomas Bohm.
2nd edition released in 2012 (improved content, design and materials).

No part of this book may be reproduced in any form, by print, electronic, or any other means without permission from the publisher.
     Reviewer (news) permissions, please only reproduce the pages and illustration that are shown at www.userdesign.co.uk/books.

Initial reference for the text content: Oxford English Mini Dictionary, 5th edition, 2003, Oxford University Press, Oxford, UK.

Cover paper: Olin Smooth Cream, 350g/m², from Antalis McNaughton, UK. Inside paper: Olin Recycled (70%) Cream, 160g/m², from Antalis McNaughton, UK. Typeface: Info. Printing: CMP, UK.

Feedback regarding this book is welcome, it can be sent to the contact details found on the website www.userdesign.co.uk/books.